Reading W
Discovery V

LEVEL 6

Manute Bol

Damian Morgan

Series Editor – Jean Conteh

While all attempts have been made to provide an accurate and balanced view of the events in this book, it must be stressed that this is an unauthorised biography of Manute Bol.

MACMILLAN

To the Teacher or Parent

This is the true story of a boy from Sudan who became a basketball star in the USA. His name was Manute Bol and, although he became rich and famous, he did not forget his family or his people in Sudan. The author, Damian Morgan, read about Manute Bol in a book. He thought the story of Manute's life was so interesting that he decided to write a book for children about it. This book will be very interesting for boys, and many girls will enjoy it, too.

The book has eight chapters.

Use the book in this way:

- Let the children read the book by themselves. Before they begin to read, make sure they know where Sudan is. Let them look at the maps on pages 3 and 47, or in an atlas or at a big map of Africa.

- As the children read, encourage them to try to work out any new words they come across.

- When the children have finished reading, ask them if they have enjoyed the story and let them discuss it with other children who have read the book.

- There are some questions and activities on pages 46–48, which will help the children to enjoy and the story more and understand it better.

Above all, let the children enjoy reading this book. Then they will want to read more books for themselves, and so become independent readers.

Chapter 1
Manute and his family

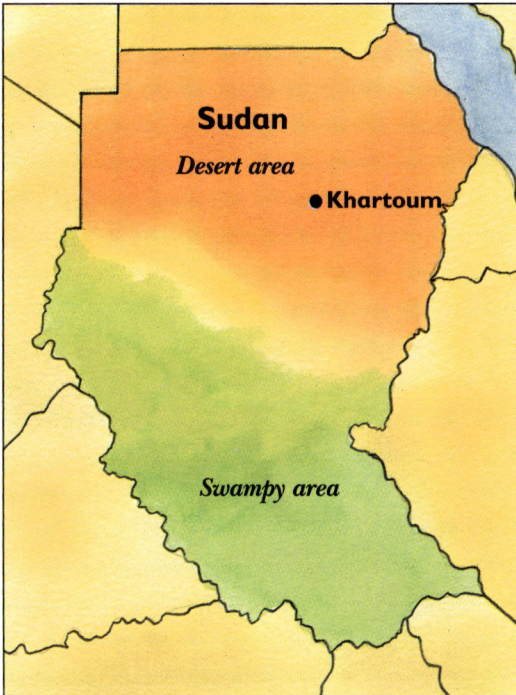

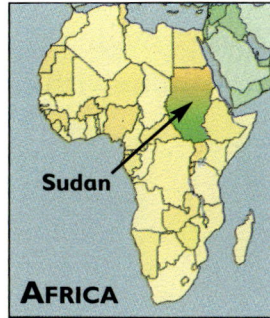

I want to tell you the story of a boy named Manute Bol. Manute Bol lived in Sudan, the largest country in Africa. He didn't live in the deserts of northern Sudan, but in the swampland of southern Sudan.

North or south, in Sudan life is hard. Many of the people who live in the swampy south of Sudan belong to the Dinka tribe.

Manute Bol was a Dinka boy. The Dinka people call themselves *monyjang*, which means 'men of men' in their language, because they are a proud people.

The Dinka people keep cows. They know how to look after cows very well. A good Dinka man takes great care of his cows. A Dinka man is rich when he has many cows.

Cows provide the Dinka with many things. They provide them with food – milk, cheese, and blood.

The Dinka use cow dung when they build their houses and as fuel for cooking. They cover themselves in cow dung to stop insects biting them. When a cow dies, the Dinka eat the meat. They make spoons and fishing harpoons from the horns.

So you can see why the Dinka think cows are the best things in the world. Manute Bol's father owned one hundred and fifty cows.

Manute's parents were called Madut and Okwok Bol. Okwok was the second wife of Madut. Altogether, Madut Bol had seven wives. They lived in a small village called Turalie.

The village sits where the river Lol joins the river Bahr el Arab. Each rainy season, the rivers rise, so the people have to move their cows out of the village to higher ground.

Even though Turalie is a small village, Manute Bol came from a great Sudanese family. Manute's great-great grandfather was called Bol Nyuol. He was a tribal chief, a healer of the sick, and a famous judge of tribal disputes. Manute's grandfather was called Bol Chol. He was also a powerful chief.

Bol Chol was very big. He stood over 2.1 m (7 ft) and weighed more than 135 kg (300 lbs). He was very, very rich. He had more than forty wives, more than eighty children, and thousands of cattle.

For this reason, Manute Bol had many family members across southern Sudan. We will meet some of them in the story.

Manute's mother, Okwok, was very unlucky. Twice, she gave birth to stillborn twins. Madut and Okwok Bol were very worried that they might not have any children. So they visited an elder called the 'master of the fishing spear'. The master blessed them and said that Okwok would give birth to a baby boy. He gave the name for the boy: 'Manute', which means 'Special blessing'.

The master's words came true and, soon, Manute was born. When he was born, no one in the little village of Turalie wrote down the date. Manute thinks he was born in October 1963. Okwok was very pleased with her baby son Manute. Now she had a boy to look after her when she was an old woman. So Okwok Bol was very, very happy.

As a child, Manute played with his father's cows. Quickly, he learnt how to look after them. But what Manute really wanted was to go to school. He wanted to learn to read and write. There were no schools in his village. No wonder no one wrote down the date of his birthday!

Manute asked his father if he could go to school. Madut was very surprised, because the Dinka boys in the village didn't go to school. They looked after the cows.

'You will not go to school!' said Madut to Manute. 'I want you to stay with me and care for the cows.'

Manute was angry.

'I want to go to school!' he shouted. 'I want to! I want to!'

Chapter 2
Manute's teeth

Did I tell you that Manute had beautiful teeth? He was very proud of his teeth. He looked after them very well. Every day, he rubbed them with dung ashes. After every meal, he cleaned them with a stick. Manute loved his beautiful teeth.

When Manute was eight or nine years old, his father called him.

'Son,' said Madut. 'It is time you had your front teeth pulled out.'

Manute backed away from his father. He did not want to lose his teeth.

'No,' he said to his father. 'I love my teeth.'

Madut glared at his son.

'It is the Dinka way!' he said. 'Everybody knows that. You are a Dinka boy. You must have your front teeth pulled out.'

'No! I will not,' shouted Manute. 'I love my teeth. I will not!'

Manute Bol didn't trust his father. He thought that his father would grab him, hold him down and prise out his beloved front teeth. Manute was afraid. He thought and thought about what he could do. He decided to run away from home.

At first, Manute just walked away from his village. As he walked, he made a plan. He decided he would go to Abyei and attend the school there. Abyei was a town 56 km (35 miles) from Manute's village, to the north. It took Manute two days to walk from his village, Turalie, to Abyei.

When he reached Abyei, he visited a merchant who was a friend of his grandfather. Manute stayed with the merchant for one week and talked to the old man about going to school.

But one afternoon, Madut Bol burst into the house. Manute screamed. He felt very frightened of his father. But he also felt angry. Madut Bol was angry too. He was so angry that he would not talk to his son. Manute was so angry that he would not talk to his father. Madut took his son home.

When they reached home, Madut said, 'Manute, you must have your teeth removed.'

'No!' shouted Manute.

'You must!' shouted Madut.

'I will not,' replied Manute. 'I love my teeth!'

Manute was scared of his father, but he was determined to keep his teeth. He glared at his father.

'You are not a true Dinka boy!' Madut shouted.

Manute still said, 'No! I won't!'

Day after day, Manute waited for his father to knock the teeth out of his mouth, but Madut did not.

He just shook his head and said, 'If you are a true Dinka boy, you will have your teeth knocked out.'

Manute kept his teeth until he was twelve years old. Then he realised that, once again, he had to run away from home.

Chapter 3
Manute grows up

The second time Manute ran away from home was not because of his teeth. There was another reason.

One day, Madut called Manute, who was with the cattle. 'You are twelve years old,' he said.

Manute looked at his mother, who was sitting nearby. Was he twelve years old? He wasn't sure.

'Yes, father?' he replied.

'You must have your head cut,' Madut said to his son.

This meant he had to have cuts made across his forehead and around his head.

Manute screamed. At twelve years old, every Dinka boy has cuts made across his forehead. It is the Dinka way. But Manute didn't want his head cut.

He didn't want his teeth removed or his head cut, so he ran away from his village again.

This time, Manute was older and stronger. This time, he decided to walk so far away from Turalie that his father could not follow him and stop him from attending school. He kept walking north until Turalie was 240 km (150 miles) behind him. He enjoyed the walk because so many people on the way were friendly to him. There were two reasons why people were friendly.

First of all, his grandfather was a famous man. Secondly, Manute was now a very tall boy. He was very, very tall.

Manute stopped walking when he reached a town called Babanusa. Babanusa was a large town. It was a trading centre. Everyone in Babanusa spoke Arabic. Manute went to the house of another merchant friend of his grandfather.

The merchant was kind to him, and allowed him to stay. But when Manute tried to attend school, he found that everyone there spoke Arabic. Manute couldn't speak Arabic, so he couldn't go to school.

Manute helped the merchant for a year. As the days passed, he started to feel guilty. He kept hearing his father's words in his head.

'You are not a true Dinka man because your teeth are in your mouth and your head is not scarred. Manute, you are not a true Dinka man.'

At night, before he went to sleep, and in his dreams, Manute heard his father's words.

'Manute, you are not a true Dinka.'

More and more, Manute thought of his mother and his little sister, Abuc. He loved his mother and sister.

Slowly, he realised that he loved his father, too. After a long, lonely year, he decided to return home.

Manute waited until the dry season, so that walking in the swampy land was easier. At first, he walked slowly because he knew his father would be angry. He wanted to keep on walking slowly, but his legs began to move fast.

His legs wanted to see his mother, his sister and his father. He walked faster and faster. He slowed down as he approached his village. His father and sister ran to welcome him, but not his mother. He searched his father's face.

'Your mother has died,' Madut said.

Manute bowed his head. He had run away from home and his mother had died. He should have been at home to look after her. He felt guilty again, sad and guilty.

He walked around the village. When he tried to talk to the girls, they laughed at him.

'Yes, you will,' Madut Bol said. 'I am your father and I order you to.'

Manute wanted to run away. But he looked at Abuc, his sister. What if she died when he was away? So he obeyed his father. For months, Manute drank only milk. He grew fat.

But, after a while, Manute lost all the milk fat. The *toc* had not worked. Manute was still thin, but he was very, very tall.

In 1978, a national politician came to Turalie. He saw Manute. He had never seen such a tall boy. A photographer from a national newspaper came to Turalie and took a photo of Manute.

Manute's cousin, Nyuol Makwag Bol, lived in Khartoum. Nyuol saw Manute's photo in the newspaper and remembered his cousin. Nyuol was a guard* on Sudan's national basketball team. He was one of the best players in the country.

He wrote to Manute.

guard: the guard on a basketball team is a shorter, quicker player who plays at the front to stop the opponents from getting the ball into the basket area.

'Manute, you are so tall,' he wrote in his letter. 'You should play basketball!'

Manute's uncle, Dr Arop, spoke to the chief of police in the southern town of Wau, which was near Turalie. The police chief invited Manute to play for the police team in Wau. Manute's father did not like it.

'Manute!' he said. 'It is your job to stay at home.'

Manute hesitated.

Manute's uncle, Dr Arop, told him that a boy who was so tall should play basketball. So Manute walked the 80 km (50 miles) to Wau, and was surprised to find it such a big city. He walked around the city. The city children followed Manute because he was so tall. When they laughed at him, he shouted at them and threw stones at them until they ran away.

The police chief said he would pay Manute to play basketball.

Manute's father followed him to Wau. He was angry with his son.

'Manute!' he said. 'You will not play basketball. You must take care of the cows.'

Manute went home with his father.

Joseph Victor Bol Bol was another of Manute's cousins. He was a pilot with Sudan Airways. He travelled to Turalie and told Manute that he could be rich and famous and live in the United States of America.

Madut Bol glared at Joseph and Manute.

'Basketball is not good work for a Dinka,' he said.

But Joseph tried to persuade Manute to go.

'Manute, Manute,' he whispered. 'You could make a lot of money if you played basketball.'

In the end Manute ignored his father's shouting and his sister's tears, and walked back to Wau.

It was November of 1979, and Manute was sixteen years old (probably). He started to practise basketball with the police team.

His cousin, Joseph Victor Bol Bol, tried to encourage him.

'Why don't you try to dunk*?' he asked.

So Manute took the ball and jumped up and dunked it. When he came down, he ripped another tooth from his mouth. Now seven teeth were gone!

---

*dunk: dunking is jumping up and putting the ball into the basket from above. The basket is more than 3 metres – exactly 10 feet – up in the air.

Manute lost six teeth to be a Dinka man. He lost another tooth to be a basketball player. From the moment he lost his tooth, he began to play basketball seriously.

Nyuol Makwag Bol, his famous basketballing cousin from Khartoum, came to visit him.

'Manute,' he said, 'Nobody famous plays basketball in Wau. Come to Khartoum with me. Then you will be famous. You will make a lot of money.'

Manute thought of his father and sister.

He thought of the money.

He travelled with Nyuol in the train to Khartoum, a distance of 960 km (600 miles).

Chapter 5

Manute in Khartoum

Khartoum is an Arab city in the desert part of Sudan. In Khartoum, the men wear turbans and *djellabas* (long gowns) and speak Arabic. The streets are hot and noisy, and nothing like the cities of southern Sudan.

Manute felt unhappy living in Khartoum. The people of Khartoum didn't like Manute, either. When he went to the market, people stopped their cars and laughed at him. When he walked down the street, he could look over the two-metre walls into the gardens of the houses. People thought he was doing this on purpose, and shouted at him. He shouted back.

Manute had a bad temper, so he punched and kicked people who laughed at him.

When he travelled on the bus, he stood on the lower step so he could stand straight. The bus conductors did not want people standing there, so they tried to push Manute off the bus.

One day Manute lost his temper with a bus conductor. He pulled the conductor off the bus and hit him.

Many years later, Manute explained his bad temper.

'In my country, the people from the north call the people from the south the *abid* (slaves). If they say it to anybody, I fight them.'

Manute joined a basketball team sponsored by Khartoum's Catholic Club. He played very badly. The coach of the Catholic Club was called Tony Amin.

Later, Tony explained how he helped Manute.

'Because Manute was very tall, he could not control his feet,' Tony said. 'Even when he walked, he could not control his feet. At first, he could do nothing on the basketball court. Even a small player could pass by him and score.'

His cousin, Nyuol Makwag Bol, also tried to help Manute.

'Manute didn't know how to shoot a jump shot*,' Nyuol once explained. 'He couldn't jump and he didn't know how to push. In basketball, you have to know how to push.'

---

*jump shot: when a player tries to jump and shoot into the basket when he is not in the basket area.

Manute had another problem, too. He couldn't catch the ball because three fingers on his right hand wouldn't open completely. Manute had to work very hard to be a basketball player.

Slowly, Manute learnt to play defence. He learnt how to move his feet to block the path of the attacking players. He could not catch with his right hand, so he learnt to swat away the ball with his left hand. Slowly, Manute became a good defender. He became the star of the Catholic Club. No other basketball team could beat the Catholic Club.

Manute's coach, Tony Amin, had many problems with Manute. First of all, Manute needed a special bed. Amin hired a carpenter to build a bed around two and a half metres (8 ft) long. Manute wore size fifteen shoes, but there were no size fifteen shoes for sale in Khartoum. Amin wrote to two Sudanese students playing basketball in the United States. He asked them to send shoes for Manute.

Manute was very, very thin. Tony Amin had a friend who owned *El Fawal*, a café near the central bus station. Manute ate at *El Fawal* free because he was a tourist attraction. Tourists came to the café to see him.

While he ate his white beans, Nile perch, tomatoes and bread, people stared at such a tall, tall man. They didn't know or care that now he was a famous basketball player.

For two years, Manute lived in a concrete shed between two grass tennis courts at the Catholic Club. He saved some money. Then, he fell in love.

Chapter 6

Manute falls in love

One day, Manute was playing basketball at the Catholic Club. A sister of one of his Dinka friends came to watch the match. While he was playing, Manute watched the girl. He liked her.

'She was very quiet,' Manute said later. 'I don't like talking girls. I like quiet girls.'

The girl's name was Nyanhial and Manute wanted to meet her. But Nyanhial did not want to meet Manute.

'It is hard to get to know Dinka girls,' Manute said later. 'You have to take time. They want to learn about you.'

So, every day, Manute sent his friends to talk to
Nyanhial. His friends went with her to see movies and told
Nyanhial about him. Manute did not know how to write,
so his friends wrote letters for him. One day, Manute could
wait no longer. He decided to meet her face to face.

He met her on a day when there was no practice.
They met at the Catholic Club. At first, she was shy, but
then she agreed to go out with him.

'OK,' she said. 'I can go out with you. I do like you.'

Manute decided that he wanted to marry Nyanhial.
Nyanhial agreed to marry Manute. But, before a Dinka
marriage, the boy's father has to pay cows to the girl's
father.

Manute took Nyanhial away and they spent a day
together.

Nyanhial's uncle came to him with a baseball bat in
his hands.

'I will kill you,' he said. 'You took my niece.'

'I want to be her husband,' said Manute. 'I'll give you plenty of cows.'

Nyanhial's uncle took his niece back to his house.

Five months later, in March of 1982, Nyanhial's father took his daughter south to Manute's village to talk about her marriage. In the shade of a giant fig tree, Manute met his father and about fifteen elders of the Bol clan to discuss the marriage.

'I don't want you to marry this girl,' Madut Bol said. He glared at Manute. 'I don't want you to play basketball. I don't want you to live in Khartoum. I don't want you to marry this girl. Her family don't have any cows!'

'I love her. I want her to be my wife,' Manute said. He glared back at his father. 'I have money. I am a Dinka man, just like you wanted. Now I want to marry.'

'No!' shouted Madut.

For many hours, the family elders talked to Madut.

'Nyanhial's family is not rich!' said Madut. 'Why should my son marry someone from a poor family?'

Finally, Madut Bol agreed.

'All right,' he said. 'Manute can marry her. But I will pay only thirty-five cows.'

But Nyanhial's father didn't agree.

'No!' he said. 'I want fifty cows. No less than fifty cows!'

'Thirty-five!' Madut shouted. 'No more than thirty-five!'

Nyanhial's father and Madut glared at each other. Manute glared at his father. The family elders talked to Madut Bol again, but he refused to give fifty cows.

Manute could not marry Nyanhial. He returned to Khartoum. His heart hurt every time he thought of the beautiful Nyanhial. His head burst with pain every time he thought of his father.

Chapter 7

Basketball in the USA

A year later, in 1983, two things happened to change Manute's life.

First, Don Feeley, an American basketball coach, visited Khartoum to help train the Sudanese military team. When he saw Manute, he asked him to play basketball in America.

Manute agreed.

'Why not?' he said. 'My father doesn't care about me.'

Manute flew to America.

He was very tall, very thin, and could not speak English. He went to school at Cleveland State University to learn English. He practised basketball with the university team. At long last, he had achieved his ambition to go to school.

A dentist made new teeth for him. He felt happy. Now his father wouldn't stop him doing anything he wanted to.

The second thing that happened was that war broke out in Sudan. Manute's father was killed.

Guilt choked Manute. He flew to Khartoum, but could not return to Turalie and his family because of the war. He thought his sister was still alive, but he couldn't visit her. He couldn't bury his father. Feeling sad and guilty, he returned to America.

After a year, Manute went to the University of Bridgeport to play for the university.

He was a star. He averaged 22.5 points* and 13.5 rebounds** a game, and blocked*** fifteen shots a game.

But Manute wasn't a real university student, so he had to leave the university. In 1984, he played for a small club and earned money to send to his sister in Turalie.

---

*points: in basketball, you score 2 points every time you shoot a basket, and 3 points if you are outside the basket area when you score.
**rebounds: if someone else shoots and misses and the ball bounces off the back board and you shoot with it, then it is a rebound.
***blocked shot: when you stop someone else from scoring.

In 1985, he joined the Washington Bullets, a rich, powerful basketball team. The coach, Dick Motta, thought Manute was too thin and would become injured.

But Manute did not miss one game because of injury. Manute used his money to buy a car, a Ford Bronco. He had the seat moved back so he could drive it.

On the basketball court, he became a star. He led the league with three hundred and ninety-seven blocked shots, which was more than ten NBA (National Basketball Association) teams combined and the second highest total in the history of American professional basketball.

Manute was a very clumsy player.

He could not shoot very well, he tripped over his own feet and he lost the ball between his legs.

But people loved him.

Manute flew to Atlanta in the south of the United States and had his photo taken for a poster to advertise Church's Fried Chicken.

He smiled at the camera for two hours and earned US $12,500.

Luckily, he had his new teeth in his mouth when the photograph was taken.

But Manute still liked to fight. Jawann Oldham, a centre for the Chicago Bulls, shoved and punched Manute on court.

Manute lost his temper and punched Oldham so hard that he fell to the floor. Two players had to hold Manute down.

'If he didn't hit me, I wouldn't fight,' said Manute, after the game.

Manute was rich now. He lived in a beautiful house. He kept the house clean.

'I don't want a basketball fan coming to my house and seeing a mess,' he said.

He always ate at a restaurant, because a Dinka man did not belong in the kitchen.

Chapter 8

Manute's marriage

Manute was successful in the USA, but he kept thinking of his family in Sudan. Because of the war, he could not go to his home village. Also, he was depressed because he had no children. He was far from home, but he was still a Dinka man.

'I'm really lonely,' he said. 'I need a wife and kids. I want somebody I can talk to. I want somebody to live with me and take care of the house.'

When the basketball season ended in 1987, he flew to Khartoum to look for a Dinka girl. Because of the war, there were not many girls. Also, many girls thought Manute was too tall.

For two months, his cousin, Natalina, searched for a girl.

Finally, Natalina found Atong, an eighteen-year-old girl from near Turalie. Atong's father was a policeman in the town of Wau. He had known Manute's father. Manute liked Atong.

Manute had plenty of money, so he agreed to pay Atong's father eighty cows, which was a very high price.

After Manute and Atong were married, they flew to Washington and Manute stopped eating at the restaurant. However, the new coach of the Washington Bullets did not think Manute was a good basketball player.

In 1988, Manute transferred to the Golden State Warriors, a team in Oakland, California. At first, he wondered if his career as a basketball player might be coming to an end.

But his new coach treated Manute well. Manute started to play the best basketball of his life. He earned a lot of money, but he didn't save it.

Manute realised that his father was right. He was a Dinka man.

So he bought two big houses in Khartoum for all his relatives who had lost their cows in the war. About forty people stayed in the houses.

Manute stopped drinking beer. Until then, he had enjoyed beer, but now he gave it up.

Manute playing with the Golden State Warriors.

'I just drank beer to have fun,' he said, later. 'But I've stopped now. People are dying back home in Sudan, because of the war, and I need to send a lot of money home. I don't save my money. I can always get more money, but you can't get more people. We Dinka people help each other a lot.'

In May, Atong gave birth to a daughter. Manute was very happy – until he heard that his sister, Abuc, was missing.

Manute wondered why, every time he became happy, his family suffered.

So that is the story of Manute Bol.

Manute is the tallest player in the history of the National Basketball Association. He has a flat-footed reach of 3.12 m (10 ft 3 ins). From fingertip to fingertip his span is almost 2.5 m (8 ft).

Manute used his height and his brains and his courage to become a star in a faraway country, but he did not forget his family or his people in Sudan.

Activity page

1 Opposite, there is a map of Sudan. Can you find the names of all the countries next to Sudan? Write a list of them. Can you find these places?

- Manute Bol's home village.
- The place he walked to when he was eight or nine years old.
- The place he walked to when he was twelve years old.
- The place where he played basketball for the Catholic Club.
- The place where his wife Atong's father worked as a policeman.

Look back in the book if you have forgotten the names of the places.

2 Manute's father was well over 2 m tall (6 ft 8 ins) but Manute grew to 2.3 m (nearly 7 ft 7 ins). How tall are you? How much taller is Manute than you? Mark your height on a wall. Mark Manute's height next to it, and his father's. You may need to stand on a chair or a box!

3 Look back in the book to find the meaning of these words. (You may have to look at the footnotes at the bottom of the pages.)

- dunk shot
- jump shot
- block shot
- rebound

LIBYA

EGYPT

Red Sea

CHAD

● Khartoum

SUDAN

ERITREA

● Babanusa

River Bahr el Arab

◉ Abyei

River Lol

● Turalie

● Wau

ETHIOPIA

CENTRAL
AFRICAN
REPUBLIC

DEMOCRATIC REPUBLIC
OF CONGO

UGANDA

KENYA

4 Have you seen people playing basketball, or have you played it yourself? It is a very exciting game. Here are some photos of African basketball players. Write down the reasons you would (or would not) like to be a full-time basketball player.

Soumalia Samake (top left)
Olumide Oyedeji (top right)
Hakeem Olajuwon (bottom)